THE
POSITIVE
DOG

THE POSITIVE DOG

A Story About the Power of *Positivity*

JON GORDON

WILEY
John Wiley & Sons, Inc.

Copyright © 2012 by Jon Gordon. All rights reserved.

Published by John Wiley & Sons, Inc., Hoboken, New Jersey.
Published simultaneously in Canada.

No part of this publication may be reproduced, stored in a retrieval system, or transmitted in any form or by any means, electronic, mechanical, photocopying, recording, scanning, or otherwise, except as permitted under Section 107 or 108 of the 1976 United States Copyright Act, without either the prior written permission of the Publisher, or authorization through payment of the appropriate per-copy fee to the Copyright Clearance Center, Inc., 222 Rosewood Drive, Danvers, MA 01923, (978) 750-8400, fax (978) 646-8600, or on the web at www.copyright.com. Requests to the Publisher for permission should be addressed to the Permissions Department, John Wiley & Sons, Inc., 111 River Street, Hoboken, NJ 07030, (201) 748-6011, fax (201) 748-6008, or online at http://www.wiley.com/go/permissions.

Limit of Liability/Disclaimer of Warranty: While the publisher and author have used their best efforts in preparing this book, they make no representations or warranties with respect to the accuracy or completeness of the contents of this book and specifically disclaim any implied warranties of merchantability or fitness for a particular purpose. No warranty may be created or extended by sales representatives or written sales materials. The advice and strategies contained herein may not be suitable for your situation. You should consult with a professional where appropriate. Neither the publisher nor author shall be liable for any loss of profit or any other commercial damages, including but not limited to special, incidental, consequential, or other damages.

For general information on our other products and services or for technical support, please contact our Customer Care Department within the United States at (800) 762-2974, outside the United States at (317) 572-3993 or fax (317) 572-4002.

Wiley publishes in a variety of print and electronic formats and by print-on-demand. Some material included with standard print versions of this book may not be included in e-books or in print-on-demand. If this book refers to media such as a CD or DVD that is not included in the version you purchased, you may download this material at http://booksupport.wiley.com. For more information about Wiley products, visit www.wiley.com.

Library of Congress Cataloging-in-Publication Data:

Gordon, Jon, 1971-
    The positive dog : a story about the power of positivity / Jon Gordon. —1
    p. cm.
  ISBN 978-0-470-88855-1 (hardback); ISBN 978-1-118-22109-9 (ebk);
  ISBN 978-1-118-23486-0 (ebk); ISBN 978-1-118-25948-1 (ebk)
    1. Motivation (Psychology) 2. Positive psychology. I. Title.
  BF503.G667 2012
  158.1—dc23

                                                  2012005817

Printed in the United States of America
SKY10028458_072721

*For Dharma,
my positive dog*

Contents

Introduction	ix
Matt and Bubba	1
The Benefits of Being Positive	5
Simple as a Smile	9
Feed with Laughter	13
Take a Thank-You Walk	17
Build Your Gratitude Muscle	19
A Day of Gratitude	23
Tell Yourself Positive Stories	27
Get to* instead of *Have to	33
Blessed* instead of *Stressed	35
Turn Complaints into Solutions	39
Fear or Faith	43

Challenges or Opportunities	**47**
An Opportunity	**49**
The Positive Dog Grows	**53**
Positive Energy is Contagious	**57**
Positive Boomerang	**59**
Feeding Others	**63**
Love	**65**
Encouragement	**67**
No Ordinary Day	**71**
Negativity Serves a Purpose	**73**
What Would Bubba Do?	**77**
A Special Day	**81**
Two Positive Dogs are Better than One	**83**
Feed the Positive Dog: Action Plan	*87*
The Positive Pledge	*97*
Resources	*99*
Feed Your Team with Positivity	*101*
About the Illustrator	*103*

Introduction

I'm not a naturally positive person. People think I am because of the books I write, but the truth is I have to work really hard at being positive. I'm a student first and a teacher second, and the student in me tries to learn and practice everything I teach. In fact, many years ago in my quest to be more positive I read all of the research in the emerging field of positive psychology and ultimately wrote a book to help people cultivate more positivity and energy in just 10 minutes a day.

Long before books such as *The Happiness Advantage, Happiness Project, Stumbling on Happiness,* and *Positivity,* I created a positive energy plan that I implemented in my own life and shared with others. Robert Emmons, the leading researcher on the impact of gratitude and a major contributor to the field of positive psychology, wrote this about my book, *The 10 Minute Energy Solution*: "Drawing on the latest scientific research, Gordon convincingly makes the case for an evidence based approach for energetic living. Just reading the book increased my energy."

However, for several reasons, including the title, the book didn't reach as many people as I hoped. I remember being at a book fair to sign copies and sitting next to me was John Grogan who was signing copies of his book *Marley and Me*. I had 10 people in line. He had hundreds of people in a line that stretched outside the building. At the time I smiled and thought, "One day I'm going to write a story about a dog that becomes more positive." So this book has been many years in the making and I'm thankful you have it in your hands.

Since my initial idea to write this book many years ago there has been an abundance of new research in the maturing field of positive psychology. Much of this research demonstrates the benefits of being positive … and following this introduction you can read eleven of these benefits. But perhaps you are someone that is motivated more by negative consequences rather than positive benefits. In this case, I have also included research that reveals the cost of negativity as well. My hope is that knowing the benefits of being positive and the cost of negativity will inspire you to read this story and implement the action plan in the back of the book.

I know there are some who may not think this book is serious enough, complicated enough, big enough, or valuable enough because it's a story about a dog that learns to be more positive and, yes, the dog talks. But please don't underestimate the message in this book because it features pictures and talking dogs. ☺

At my company, one of our core principles is *simple is powerful*, and I have shared the simple, powerful strategies in this book with Fortune 500 companies, professional sports teams, college football teams that have played in national championships, school districts, and hospitals—and I know they work. The proof is in the thousands of emails I have received from people sharing with me how these strategies have influenced their life and work. The strategies in this book have grown sales revenue, motivated salespeople, improved team performance, developed positive kids, enhanced careers, improved marriages, and lead to greater individual and team success.

The goal of this book is to take much of the research on positivity and make it simple, fun, and actionable so anybody, even a child, can benefit from feeding the positive dog. In this spirit, I hope you enjoy the book, have fun with the story, follow the action plan, and experience the benefits of being positive. Like me, you may not be naturally positive, but as the research shows, you can become more positive and improve the direction and quality of your life.

11 Benefits of Being Positive

1. Positive people live longer. In a study of nuns, those that regularly expressed positive emotions lived an average of 10 years longer than those who didn't (Snowdon, 2001).
2. Positive work environments outperform negative work environments (Goleman, 2011).
3. Positive, optimistic salespeople sell more than pessimistic salespeople (Seligman, 2006).
4. Positive leaders are able to make better decisions under pressure (Institute of HeartMath, 2012).
5. Marriages are much more likely to succeed when the couple experiences a 5-to-1 ratio of positive to negative interactions, whereas when the ratio approaches 1-to-1, marriages are more likely to end in divorce (Gottman, 1999).
6. Positive people who regularly express positive emotions are more resilient when facing stress, challenges, and adversity.
7. Positive people are able to maintain a broader perspective and see the big picture, which helps them identify solutions, whereas negative people maintain a narrower perspective and tend to focus on problems (Fredrickson, 2009).

8. Positive thoughts and emotions counter the negative effects of stress. For example, you can't be thankful and stressed at the same time.
9. Positive emotions such as gratitude and appreciation help athletes perform at a higher level (Institute of HeartMath, 2012).
10. Positive people have more friends, which is a key factor of happiness and longevity (Putnam, 2000).
11. Positive and popular leaders are more likely to garner the support of others and receive pay raises and promotions and achieve greater success in the workplace.

More research and links to studies and resources can be found at www.feedthepositivedog.com.

The Costs of Negativity

1. Ninety percent of doctor visits are stress related, according to the Centers for Disease Control and Prevention.
2. A study found that negative employees can scare off every customer they speak with—for good (Rath, 2004).
3. At work, too many negative interactions compared to positive interactions can decrease the productivity of a team, according to Barbara Fredrickson's research at the University of Michigan.
4. Negativity affects the morale, performance, and productivity of our teams.
5. One negative person can create a miserable office environment for everyone else.
6. Robert Cross's research at the University of Virginia demonstrates that 90 percent of anxiety at work is created by 5 percent of one's network—the people who sap energy.
7. Negative emotions are associated with decreased life span and longevity.
8. Negative emotions increase the risk of heart attack and stroke.

9. Negativity is associated with greater stress, less energy, and more pain.
10. Negative people have fewer friends.

More research and links to studies and resources can be found at www.feedthepositivedog.com.

THE
POSITIVE
DOG

Matt and Bubba

His name was Matt but they called him Mutt and a shelter was his home. He had a tough life before being rescued and brought to the shelter. Perhaps that's why he was so mad and sad and often barked as people came to look at him.

"He's mean. Let's pick another doggy," the children would say to their parents as they walked away from his cage.

"Where you going?" Matt would say, but it was too late. They were gone and Matt was left wondering why he had no one to love and no one to love him.

He often walked around the yard during play time and complained to anyone who would listen. He complained about his past. He complained about being at the shelter. He complained that his life wasn't what he dreamed it would be when he was a young pup. When he grew tired of complaining he would just lie down by himself, think of all the sad events from the past, and feel depressed.

One day while walking around the yard feeling sorry for himself he came across Bubba, the big dog who was walking around singing his favorite song about a dog uniting with his owner.

Bubba loved country music, fresh cold air, positive psychology, movies with happy endings, and most of all, helping the hopeless find hope. He smiled at the little dog who approached him and wondered if he'd ever seen anything more hopeless. He knew someone had to teach this dog how to hunt for the *good* things in life. Besides, he had made a pact: One day, not long ago, Bubba woke up to find his house on fire. Trapped in the maze of flames and smoke, he promised that if he made it out alive, he would help everyone and anyone he could.

"What's up little mutt? What's got you so down?" Bubba asked the sad, little dog.

"Oh, a bunch of things," said Matt. "I've got one problem bigger than the next. I've got so many big problems, I don't know which one is the biggest."

"I do," said Bubba as he put his paw on Matt's shoulder. "Since our cages are right across from each other, I've been watching you for a while now and I definitely know your biggest problem."

"You do?" said Matt as his eyes opened wider.

"Yep," said Bubba. "It's so clear, but you can't see it because you are blinded by negativity. Your biggest problem is that you are feeding the negative dog inside you. You see, we all have two dogs inside of us. One dog is positive, happy, optimistic, and hopeful. The other dog is negative, mad, sad, pessimistic, and fearful. These two dogs often fight inside us but guess who wins the fight?"

Matt looked confused. "I don't know, Bubba," he said as he shook his head.

"The dog who wins is the one you feed the most," Bubba exclaimed. "You have to feed the positive dog inside you and starve the negative dog. The more you feed the positive dog, the more it grows. The more you starve the negative dog, the more it shrinks and weakens. You become the dog you feed, so feed the positive dog and your *big* problems will give way to big blessings and a bright future."

Bubba then playfully tagged Matt and off they ran to play around the yard and talk about the power and benefits of positivity and the costs of negativity.

The Benefits of Being Positive

"It's one thing to say you need to feed the positive dog. It's another thing to truly understand why you should be positive in the first place," Bubba said as he stopped under a large tree and began to dig. After a few minutes he lowered his head in the hole and, using his nose, he scooped up a large book that had been buried underneath the dirt.

"This is a book that was left by Jade, one of the college students that volunteered at the shelter a few months ago," said Bubba. "She was a pretty, young thing and not only did she smell real nice but she would also read the book out loud to us during quiet time. I learned all about the latest research on the positive effects of being positive and the negative effects of being negative from her and this here book. In fact, I've read the book so much I pretty much have it memorized. And you know what?"

"What?" asked Matt who was really curious to learn what Bubba knew.

"The research is clear," Bubba proclaimed. "It really does pay to be positive. Positivity makes us happier and healthier. It helps us live longer and improves our relationships. It makes us better leaders and leads to greater success. Being positive is not just a nice way to live. It's the *best* way to live. Best of all, the research doesn't just apply to humans. It also applies to dogs because, as everyone knows, dogs have thoughts and feel emotions, too.

"Not only does it pay to be positive," Bubba continued, "but the research says that there are also big costs to being negative. For example, negative emotions increase our risk of having a heart attack and stroke. Negativity weakens our immune system, makes us feel more stressed, and saps our energy. It is also associated with feeling more depressed and making fewer friends. The simple truth is that no one wants to be around a negative person or dog," Bubba said, knowing Matt needed to hear it.

"I guess that's why no one wants to be around me or take me home," Matt said as he put his head down and started to cry. "That's why I'm still here at the shelter."

"Well, that's probably true," said Bubba as he put his paw on Matt's head. "I ain't going to lie to you. Your attitude certainly hasn't been one that would win friends and influence people in a positive way. But the great news is that now you know the benefits of being positive and the costs of being negative. And now that you *know* the importance of being positive you can *be* positive.

"You don't have to be mad and sad anymore. You don't have to focus on your problems. You don't have to feel sorry for yourself. You can feed the positive dog and starve the negative dog on your way to a happier, successful, and more fulfilled life. You can be the kind of positive dog that every dog in the shelter wants to be around and every family wants to take home."

Matt looked up at Bubba as his eyes opened wider. For the first time in a long time he felt a sense of hope. Bubba gave him a vision for his life and everything he said felt like the truth. He didn't want people to walk away from his cage anymore. He didn't want children to think he was mean. He wanted to love and be loved. He wanted to enjoy all the benefits that came from being positive. Most of all he wanted a family to fall in love with him and take him home. If he could be more positive, then perhaps his dream could come true.

As playtime ended, Barry, the man in charge of the shelter, called the dogs back into the building. Bubba nosed Jade's book back into the hole and covered it with dirt, for safekeeping. As they headed inside, Matt decided he was ready to start feeding the positive dog inside him.

"Is it hard to feed the positive dog?" he asked.

"It's a lot easier and simpler than you think," Bubba said. "Tomorrow, first thing in the morning, we'll begin our positive feast and your life will never be the same!"

Simple as a Smile

"Feeding the positive dog doesn't happen unless you take action," Bubba said as he and Matt walked around the yard the next morning. "It's something that you must intentionally do each day. When you make it a habit you not only change how you think and feel but you also literally change how your brain works. The research shows that we can actually mold our brains to be more positive by feeding them positivity each day."

"How do you do this?" Matt asked, thinking the answer was going to be complicated and difficult.

"It's as simple as a smile," said Bubba as they stopped to smell some flowers. "Smiling has the same effect as smelling these here beautiful flowers. It makes you feel good."

"But what if I don't feel like smiling?" Matt said as he tried to recall the last time he actually smiled.

"Well that's the thing," Bubba answered. "Too often we wait for something in life to make us smile. We wait until we feel positive and a smile happens. But you don't have to wait to feel positive enough for a smile to happen. You can generate a positive feeling by smiling. Your smile can be the source of your positivity, not just the result of it." Bubba then lifted his nose and inhaled the fresh cold air, paused for a moment, and said, "When you think of smiling remember this: Waiting for something to make you smile is like sitting in a dark room waiting for someone to turn on the light switch. But making yourself smile is like turning on a light switch inside you. You have the power to make yourself feel good. In fact, when you smile you produce more serotonin in your brain—serotonin is an antidepressant that makes you feel happier and more positive."

"Does everyone know this?" Matt asked. This was the first time he had heard of anything like this.

"No they don't," Bubba answered. "Most people and dogs don't have a clue about this. They underestimate the power of a smile. They don't realize that within us we have a 100 percent, all natural drug we can give ourselves anytime we want to feel good—and it's as simple as a smile."

"Like this?" Matt said as he struggled to move his mouth to form a smile. "I'm smiling but I don't really feel any better. Maybe I don't have any serotonin in me."

"That's not it," Bubba said. "The trick is, it has to be a real smile for it to work. Fake smiles don't produce serotonin in your brain. In fact, the research shows that fake smiles and fake positivity can be harmful and cause stress. Only a real smile will make you feel good. You were smiling just with your mouth but a real smile involves your eyes too. A real smile shines from the heart through the eyes, lights up every cell in your body, and radiates outward for the world to see."

Bubba then started tickling Matt and for the first time in a long time Matt actually smiled.

Feed with Laughter

"Now *that's* a smile!" Bubba cheered as he touched Matt's mouth with his paw. "I knew you had it in you."

"I haven't smiled in so long I forgot what it feels like," Matt said.

"And how does it feel?"

"It feels good—really good."

"Yep," Bubba said. "A smile is only a laugh away. If you want to smile more, then laugh more. If you want to generate real smiles, then think of things that make you laugh like this here joke: Knock, knock."

"Who's there?" Matt asked.

"Dog."

"Dog who?"

"Doggonit, why aren't you answering the door?"

All at once Bubba and Matt burst out with laugher, fell to the grass, and rolled around on their backs as they continued to laugh uncontrollably. They laughed and laughed and laughed and when they stopped laughing Bubba told another joke and they laughed some more.

Eventually they calmed down and got to their feet. Matt said, "Wow, I don't ever remember smiling or feeling like this. I feel like I can fly."

"Yep, laughter not only makes you smile more, it's also a powerful way to feed the positive dog each day," Bubba said. "Studies show that laughter improves your mood, reduces stress, boosts your immune system, relaxes your muscles, and adds joy to your life. Laughing is a priceless, free drug you can feed yourself anytime you want to feel positive. Best of all, you don't have to wait for something to make you laugh, you can think of funny experiences or jokes to get the ball rolling."

Bubba then started digging and once again scooped out Jade's book and showed Matt a story about a man named Norman Cousins who was diagnosed with a painful illness for which there was no cure. Instead of accepting his fate he became the subject of his own experiment. He decided to fill his body and brain with tons of positive emotions by watching hours of Marx Brothers movies and having his nurse read him humorous stories. He discovered that a ten minute, hearty belly laugh could help him sleep two hours without pain and in a short time he was off painkillers and sleeping pills. Cousins declared that he laughed himself to health and that laughter is a good way to jog internally without having to go outdoors.

"If he can do it," Bubba said, "so can you. You can make yourself laugh and generate real smiles with humorous thoughts."

"It's all about our thoughts, isn't it?" Matt asked as he was beginning to grasp how feeding the positive dog works.

"Yes it is," Bubba said as Barry called for all the dogs to come into the shelter. It was nap time, but as the other dogs made their way into their kennels and went to sleep, Matt stayed awake and remembered the funny jokes Bubba told

Feed with Laughter

him and once again laughed and smiled. He also thought of the lessons Bubba taught him and knew he would remember them better if he imagined they were written on dog bones like this:

Positive or Negative: Whichever one you feed grows.

Positive dogs live longer, happier and healthier lives.

Feed the positive dog with real smiles and big laughs!

Take a Thank-You Walk

The next morning as Bubba and Matt walked around the yard, Bubba explained that it's not just humorous thoughts that feed our positive dog. We can also feed the positive dog inside us with thoughts of gratitude and appreciation.

"One of my favorite things to do is practice gratitude while taking my morning walk. I call it a thank-you walk, and ever since I've been doing it I've become more positive," said Bubba.

"How do you do it?" Matt asked.

"It's really simple, little buddy. While you are walking you just think of all the things that you are thankful for. You think of all the positive things about your life."

"So, right now I shouldn't be thinking about how this walk would be a whole lot better if I was with a boy who considered me his family dog?" Matt asked.

"No, no, no, you shouldn't," Bubba answered. "You don't want to start your day thinking about what you *don't* have and *don't* like. That only feeds the negative dog. You want to start your day thinking about what is good in your life, what you are thankful for, what you appreciate."

"Like what?" Matt asked as he tried to think of something that was good in his life.

"Well, I think of the fact that I was able to escape from a burning house and of how thankful I am to be alive. Of course, I miss my home and I miss the family I had, but I try to cherish what I have rather than think about what I don't. I give thanks for being alive, for being able to walk, for the ability to smell beautiful flowers and inhale fresh cold air. I find that the more I'm thankful for the little things, the more at peace I feel and the more positive I am. I also find that when I'm taking a thank-you walk, I don't feel stressed. The research in Jade's book supports this. It shows that *you can't be stressed and thankful at the same time*, so if you are practicing gratitude, you can't be stressed. When you are grateful, you also flood your brain and body with positive emotions and natural antidepressants that uplift you rather than the stress hormones that drain you. So a thank-you walk is a great way to start the day, create the right mindset, and feed the positive dog first thing in the morning."

Build Your Gratitude Muscle

"But what about the rest of the day?" Matt asked. "Can I take a thank-you walk during the day, too?"

"Great question. You're a lot smarter than you look," said Bubba before laughing. "Of course. You can take a thank-you walk any time of day."

"Good," said Matt, "because sometimes I feel too tired in the morning."

"I understand that little buddy and while you can take a thank-you walk any time I encourage you to make it a habit in the morning because there is nothing more energizing than walking and practicing gratitude at the same time. A morning thank-you walk gives you a double boost of positivity to start your day.

"It's also important to know that you can practice gratitude throughout your entire day—even when you are standing still. When you wake up in the morning you can think about the things you are grateful for. You can say

I'm thankful for a roof over my head, I'm thankful that I am not sleeping in the freezing cold outside. You can practice gratitude when you are eating breakfast and give thanks for the food and water that nourish your body. You can be thankful that you can walk and smell and hear and see. You can be thankful for lunchtime and nap time, playtime and sleep time. And when you are going to sleep at night, you can be thankful for all the great events of the day. You can think about your favorite success of the day—the one thing or person that made you smile, laugh, and feel great—and you can be grateful it happened."

"Wow, it seems like you can be grateful for anything," Matt said. "Do you ever run out of things to be thankful for?"

"Never," said Bubba. "When you are grateful for the gifts in your life, big and small, you always find more things to be grateful about. I have also found that *abundance flows into your life when gratitude flows out of your heart.* You become a gratitude magnet and attract more good fortune, joy, love, peace, happiness, and positivity so your list of things to be grateful about keeps growing."

"But it doesn't happen unless I do it, right?" asked Matt.

"That's right," Bubba answered. "*Gratitude is like muscle. The more we do with it the stronger it gets.* So to build your gratitude muscle, what I want you to do today is to identify all the things, even small things, you are grateful for. Even when a negative thought or complaint comes into your mind I want you to replace it with gratitude. For example if you don't like the meal Barry serves today, you can be thankful that at least you have some food to eat while there are so many starving dogs in the world. Gratitude is a choice and you can feed the positive dog inside you all day long if you are ready and willing."

"I'm ready and willing," said Matt.

"Great," said Bubba. "I'm going to go talk to a few other dogs on the other side of the yard that could use some positivity. Remember all the things we talked about, do your best to build your gratitude muscle today and we'll talk about it tonight."

A Day of Gratitude

The first thing Matt did was to remember some of the important lessons Bubba shared with him.

> You can't be stressed and thankful at the same time.

> Gratitude is like muscle. The more you do with it, the stronger it gets.

> Abundance flows into your life when gratitude flows out of your heart.

Matt then walked over to the water bowl and gave thanks while he drank some water. Then, he looked around and was thankful he had such a big yard to run and play in. He took off running and was thankful for legs to run and the grass to run on. He joined a few of the other young mutts and was thankful he had friends to play with.

As the hours passed he found more and more things to be thankful for. Bubba was right. The more grateful you are, the more you get things to be grateful about. He noticed that at first it felt awkward to be grateful about such small things but the more often he did it, the more natural it felt. He figured the awkwardness was the result of an underdeveloped gratitude muscle which was now getting stronger.

His biggest test came when a family visited the shelter to choose a dog to take home. They came by his kennel and commented on how cute he was, but they ended up choosing another dog. He was upset and angry, but remembered Bubba's advice and decided to be grateful for the fact that it was the first time people stayed at his cage and didn't call him mean. He did his best to smile and laugh instead of bark and he was thankful that it made a difference. Instead of running away, they actually stayed and petted him for a little while. He was thankful that, perhaps, this meant he was on his way to getting adopted one day.

He told all of these experiences to Bubba as they lay in their kennels that night and Bubba just smiled, knowing that his little friend now had a big appetite for positivity. He was glad that Matt experienced firsthand what every positive dog knows: That feeding the positive dog really does make a difference, and gratitude is the ultimate food for those who want to be more positive.

Matt then paused for a moment and cleared his throat. "Speaking of gratitude, Bubba, I want to tell you what my success of the day was. Well actually it's the best thing that's ever happened to me," he said with a big smile on his face.

"What's that, little buddy?" asked Bubba.

"Meeting and spending time with you," Matt said before closing his eyes and falling asleep.

Tell Yourself Positive Stories

The rain poured down as Bubba and Matt walked around the yard the next morning. "So how do you like the rain?" Bubba asked.

"Oh, I love it," Matt said enthusiastically. "I love getting all wet and then shaking the water off my body."

"I feel the same way. I also love how the rain cleanses everything. But you know, not everyone feels the way we do," Bubba said while pointing to another dog across the yard. "See Niro over there. He hates the rain. Always yells and gets angry when it rains—grumbles that he's all wet and sticky."

"It's interesting that two dogs can experience the same event and perceive it very differently," Matt said.

"Yep," said Bubba. "One dog loves the rain; the other dog hates it. Their perspectives determine their thoughts, feelings, and, ultimately, how they act for the rest of the day. It's like that with everything in life. How we perceive people, events, and situations determines our reality. That's why I often say that we don't live our lives based on reality. Nope. We live our lives based on our perspective and our perception of reality."

"That's why it's so important to develop a positive perspective, isn't it?" said Matt, knowing he had experienced the impact of a positive perspective firsthand. When he laughed and smiled, he changed his perspective from negative to positive. When he practiced gratitude throughout the day, instead of complaining about everything, he saw the world through the eyes of gratitude and it changed his reality.

"That's right," Bubba said. "How you see the world defines your world. So if you want to live a positive life you must feed the positive dog with positive perspectives—and I'm convinced that these positive perspectives are influenced by the positive stories we tell ourselves."

"What kind of stories?" Matt asked.

"Big stories and little stories," answered Bubba. "First off, each one of us is telling ourselves a big story—a main story that defines our life. Like in the movies, we all have a central theme and certain genre that defines our life. Some people and dogs define their lives with a negative story. For them it's a drama or a horror story. For others, their lives are like a positive movie such as a love story, adventure, or inspirational tale. It's important to identify the type of movie we are living because the story we tell ourselves defines our perspective and the lives we live."

Matt thought for a moment and tried to identify the movie he was living. He realized that his movie had been a drama but now it was becoming more of an adventure.

"Can we change our story?" asked Matt, hoping it was possible.

"Of course you can," said Bubba. "The great news is that you can change your story anytime you want from a negative story to a positive story. If you are living a drama then you can decide to change it to an adventure. If you are living a horror story you can decide to change it to an inspirational tale. Think about it: In the horror story and inspirational tale, the main character gets knocked down. In the drama the victim stays down, but in the inspirational tale the victim becomes a hero, gets back up, and armed with optimism and belief in a positive future, takes the actions necessary to create it."

It was such an important lesson that Matt wanted to be sure he'd remember, so he made a few mental notes.

> The story you tell yourself defines the life you live and the actions you take.

> It's important to tell yourself a positive story.

"It's not just big stories that create our perspective and define our life. We also define our life by all the little stories we tell ourselves every day," Bubba said.

"What are little stories?" Matt asked.

"Little stories are our *beliefs* and *philosophies* about life. You tell yourself many little stories throughout your life based on your belief system, attitude, and approach to life and these stories feed you either negatively or positively and define how you think and act. For example, one dog tells himself that he'll never make it out of the shelter, while another dog believes that it will happen when the time is right. One story is filled with despair and the other, hope. Or, consider a dog that believes in overcoming adversity to pursue her dreams, while another dog believes in settling for what life gives her. Their stories and approach to life will define their perspectives, how they live, and the lives they create. Or, consider a dog that once complained all the time but then started telling himself little stories filled with gratitude.

"Like me," said Matt.

"Just like you, Matty," said Bubba with a big smile on his face. "A few days of feeding the positive dog and you've already noticed a difference. Now imagine if you had more strategies to feed the positive dog with positive stories and perspectives. Imagine if you did this every day for the rest of your life. How much more positive would you be?"

"A lot more," said Matt who was excited to learn more.

"You bet," said Bubba. "Your positivity would soar and that's why I'm going to share some more with you. You don't have to feed yourself with negative stories and negative perspectives anymore. You can change from negative to positive as fast as I can say 'Lassie.' I have found that you can change your negative perspectives to positive perspectives by just changing or choosing a few different words. Yep, just by changing a few words you can feed the positive dog instead of the negative dog."

Get to instead of *Have to*

"One of my favorite ways to change the story you tell yourself is to say *get to* instead of *have to*," said Bubba.

"How does it work?" asked Matt.

"It's a word swap," answered Bubba. "For example, humans say the words *have to* all the time. If you hear them talk they say *I have to take the dog for a walk* or *I have to go to work* or *I have to pick up the kids*. Knowing what I know now, after reading Jade's book, I would tell them you don't have to do anything. You *get* to take me for a walk. You *get* to rub my belly, since I give you so much love while you do it. You *get* to go to a job while so many are unemployed. You *get* to pick up your children in your car, because you should be thankful that you have children."

"Wow. Changing two words really makes a difference," said Matt.

"Yep. Changing just two words can change your mindset and approach. When you change *have to* to *get to* you change a complaining voice to an appreciative heart."

"It's about gratitude, isn't it?" asked Matt.

"A lot of feeding the positive dog is about gratitude," answered Bubba. "And speaking of gratitude here's another word swap that can turn stress into appreciation."

Blessed instead of *Stressed*

"We can choose to feel *blessed* instead of *stressed*. After all, stress is one of the biggest challenges we face in life," said Bubba. "Research shows that chronic stress weakens our immune system, increases our blood pressure, drains our energy, affects our sleep, depletes feel-good neurotransmitters dopamine and serotonin, and accelerates aging, which is not a good thing since we dogs don't have much time on earth as it is. Simply put, stress wreaks havoc on our mental and physical health and it is a huge obstacle for those trying to be more positive.

"When we are stressed we activate the part of our brain associated with stress and fear and this causes us to focus on our survival. We become very territorial and our primary concern becomes our own safety. Instead of making new friends and developing positive relationships we see others as threats and we go into *fighting-angry dog mode*. This is a good thing if we are being threatened by a mean dog or human, but most of the time this is not the case and so our stress more often hurts us than helps us. The good news is that there is an antidote to stress and it is to feel blessed. When you feel blessed you can't feel stressed. When you are thankful you activate the part of your brain associated with positive emotions. You think more clearly, make better decisions and you feel better about yourself and everything in your life."

"I know. I felt this way when I practiced gratitude all day long yesterday," Matt said.

Bubba smiled. "Yep, gratitude is one of the greatest gifts we can give ourselves. While it may not be possible to practice gratitude all the time like you did yesterday, just remember that anytime you are feeling stressed you can turn it around by feeling blessed. When you count your blessings you'll reduce your stressings."

"How many blessings should I count?" asked Matt.

"As many as you want, but a very easy and practical strategy is to think of three things you are thankful for anytime you feel stressed. You'll not only reduce your stress but also feel more joy, make more friends, and gain a broader perspective of the world," said Bubba.

"How so?" asked Matt.

"Well for one thing, when you feel blessed instead of stressed, you look for friends instead of foes. You focus on what's possible instead of impossible and you focus more on solutions instead of complaints. And speaking of complaints and solutions, they are the next two words you can change to change your story," said Bubba.

Turn Complaints into Solutions

"Nothing feeds the negative dog inside you like complaining," Bubba said.

"I know," said Matt. "I'm a pretty good complainer."

"Pretty good? If complaining were in the criteria for the Westminster Kennel Club's Best in Show you would be the winner," Bubba said, before letting out a big belly laugh.

"But I'm complaining a lot less," Matt said.

"Yes, you are, and as we talked about with *get to* instead of *have to* it's important to focus on gratitude rather than complaints. But here's the deal: I don't want you to get rid of complaining completely."

"Why not?" Matt asked.

"Because, let's face it, there are times when complaining is helpful and, with the right perspective, you can turn complaints into solutions.

"How's that?" asked Matt.

"Well, instead of mindlessly complaining and venting to yourself and others, you can think of solutions to your complaints. You can make a pact with yourself that you are not going to complain unless you identify one or two solutions to your complaint. Jade called it the 'No Complaining Rule,' and she read it to us when she was here. Since then, I've adopted the rule and found that instead of letting complaining generate negative energy, we can use it for a positive purpose. We can use our own complaints as a *signal*, letting us know we are feeding the negative dog, and then, in the next moment, we can think of solutions and feed the positive dog instead. Each time we catch ourselves complaining, we can say, 'Okay, I don't like this. I'm not happy about this. So then, what do I want? What will make me happy? What thought will bring me peace instead of frustration? What positive actions can I take to rectify this complaint? What solution will address this problem?' Every complaint represents an opportunity to turn something negative into a positive and we can use complaining as a catalyst for positive change and positive action in our own lives, at work, and in the world."

"So, you are saying that there are times when I need to replace my complaints with gratitude, and there are other times when I should turn my complaints into solutions,"

Matt said, as he grasped the different strategies Bubba taught.

"Exactly," said Bubba. "The strategies I share are different foods to feed the positive dog and you can choose what food is right for you in that moment or situation."

Bubba then paused for a moment and looked up at the sky. The rain had stopped and a ray of light found its way through an opening in the clouds. He had shared several strategies to help Matt change his story and feed the positive dog, and wondered if he should share the last two strategies now or wait until tomorrow. He looked at Matt and saw the hunger for knowledge and change in his eyes and knew that he couldn't wait to share the most powerful strategies of all.

Fear or Faith

Bubba and Matt walked to the fence that surrounded the shelter's yard and looked beyond it to see the world they hoped awaited them. Bubba turned to Matt and said, "The most important decision we can make is to choose faith instead of fear. All of our negativity is rooted in fear. Complaining, anger, jealousy, and sadness are ultimately caused by fear that expresses itself in negative ways. Fear of the unknown causes us to protect the status quo when change would be beneficial for us. Fear of being powerless causes us to complain. Fear of failing leads to inaction. Fear of being hurt leads to anger. Fear of not being good, successful, or smart enough leads to jealousy. Fear of not being loved leads to sadness. Fear holds us back from living the life we were born to live. It paralyzes us from taking positive actions and makes us bark at people who come to see us, turning them away. But thankfully, there is an antidote to fear. It is faith! And what do fear and faith have in common?" asked Bubba.

"They both begin with the letter F," said Matt.

"True," said Bubba, "but I'm talking deeper than that. Faith and fear both believe in a future that hasn't happened yet. Fear believes in a negative future. Faith believes in a positive future. So I ask you, if neither the positive or negative future has happened yet, why not choose to believe in the positive future? Why not believe that great things are coming your way? Think about it. Fear says that a family will never adopt you but faith says that a family will surely adopt you in the future. Which one will you choose?"

"Faith, for sure," cheered Matt.

"You got it," Bubba said. "When you choose faith, you tap into the ultimate food source to feed the positive dog inside you. Faith helps you overcome the fear that sabotages your joy and success. It helps you get through tough times when you want to give up. Faith fills you up with hope, optimism, and inspiration. Telling yourself a story of faith changes you from a victim to a hero, and your belief in a positive future leads to powerful actions today. Because you believe in yourself and the future, you take the actions necessary to create it. Best of all faith helps you turn challenges into opportunities, which is so important because if there is one thing that can cause us to feed the negative dog it is the challenges we face in life."

Challenges or Opportunities

"No one goes through life untested," Bubba continued. "We will all face challenges in our lives. But we have a choice. We can allow these challenges to destroy us or they can make us stronger—and it is our perspective that decides the outcome. We can choose to see adversity as just a challenge or as an opportunity that helps us learn, improve, and grow." Bubba then started digging and scooped up Jade's book and read a study to prove his point. "Yep, it says here that researchers studied 500 humans in Britain who seemed to have it all—wealth, success, happiness. The researchers were surprised to learn that these very successful people all had bad things happen to them like everyone else. However, one key characteristic they all possessed was that they turned bad events into good outcomes. While they were in the midst of their challenges they looked for the opportunity and they turned misfortune into fortune.

"How do I do this?" Matt asked knowing he wanted to turn his misfortune into fortune.

"It's as simple as asking yourself a few questions," responded Bubba. "You ask: *What can I learn from this experience? How can I grow from it? What do I do now?*

"In fact, this is what I had to do when I ended up in here. One moment I was sleeping with a family I loved, and the next moment I was here. At first, I only saw the challenges before me. I wasn't interested in opportunities. Then Jade came to the shelter and started reading her book to us and I realized I needed to change my attitude. Instead of being all sad that I'm alone in a shelter, I figured I could use my time at the shelter to improve the lives of the dogs here."

"And that's why you're helping me," Matt said cheerfully.

"Yep," said Bubba. "My challenge became an opportunity to help others. I honestly don't know if someone will adopt an old, big dog like me. Of course it's possible and I have faith that if it's meant to be, it will happen, but until that day I know my opportunity is right here at this shelter and I'm making the most of it."

An Opportunity

As Bubba finished sharing his insights with Matt, Barry called all the dogs back into the shelter. They ate lunch and then went to rest in their cages while visitors came to look at them. As Matt lay in his kennel, he saw a man and woman and their two children stop in front of Bubba's door.

"He's a big, cute guy," the man said.

"Yeah, but he's too old," the woman said. "We want a dog our kids can grow up with. We need a young guy like this one here," she said as she looked into Matt's cage.

Matt wanted to bark but he didn't. He remembered to smile and think positive thoughts as she looked at him. The man followed his wife to Matt's cage and stood next to her and put his hand out. Matt reached his mouth through the opening in the cage and licked the man's hand.

"He's a cute, little guy," the man said.

Matt couldn't believe it. They were going to pick him. This was his day. He was going to be adopted. He could hardly contain his excitement.

Then he heard one of the children yell, "Mommy, Daddy! I love this doggie over here!" The parents ran over and Barry took the dog out of the cage and gave it to the child to hold. Then, Matt heard the words that didn't make him feel very positive.

"We'll take him," the man said. And Matt knew that today wasn't his day to get adopted. He looked up and saw Bubba, and they looked at each other with sadness in their eyes.

Yes, they were positive dogs, but today no one wanted them and it was okay to be sad. They had faith that it would happen when the time was right, but today just wasn't the right time. Perhaps there was more he needed to learn and do before it was time to leave the shelter. Like Bubba, Matt decided he would turn the challenge of being there into an opportunity.

An Opportunity

The Positive Dog Grows

Matt spent the next few days feeding the positive dog with the strategies Bubba taught him, and he even created some of his own. He realized that he felt very positive when he was doing something he enjoyed such as digging, playing catch with a ball, or jumping to catch Barry's Frisbee. He also felt energized when he relaxed in silence, and it occurred to him that feeding the positive dog was most powerful when he focused on the present moment.

Bubba told him that the research supported his experience. It showed that doing something you enjoy and being in the present moment are big positivity boosters—as are meditation and prayer. In fact research shows that meditation and prayer reduce stress, boost positivity, and enhance health, vitality, and longevity. Matt made mental notes of this and made it a point to practice them in his daily life.

> Prayer and meditation feed your positive dog.

> When you are doing something that interests you, you feel more positive.

> When you are playing and having fun, you feel more positive.

As the days turned into weeks, Matt discovered that the more he practiced positivity, the more open he became to everything in his life. He made more friends. He came up with many new solutions to his complaints and he created many new strategies to be more positive. He realized that the more positive he became, the more open he became; the more friends, solutions, and possibilities flowed into his life, all of which generated even more positivity. He realized that positivity doesn't just feed the positive dog inside you; it also feeds itself and grows in your life. Bubba told Matt that Jade's book mentioned a researcher named Barbara Fredrickson, and her work supported his experience. "Positivity doesn't just change you; it changes everything around you," he said.

And everything in Matt's life did change. Instead of being a constant complainer he always focused on what was *good* in his life. Instead of feeling negative and depressed he felt more positive, healthier, stronger, and more energized.

Matt also discovered a big benefit of being positive was that he was better able to handle setbacks and challenges. Time after time, people came to the shelter to select a dog, but Matt wasn't chosen. Instead of feeling rejected he chose to believe he was being protected. He came to believe that every dog has an owner that is meant for them, and the fact that he hadn't been adopted yet meant that he was being protected from being with the wrong owner. He believed he would be adopted when the right owner—the only one he was meant to be with—came to the shelter.

Matt also became more adept at overcoming minor challenges. In the past, a fight with another dog, a bad tasting meal, or an injury to his leg would have ruined his day but now Matt was able to turn adversity into a learning opportunity. Challenges still happened, but his positivity allowed him to bounce back and grow from them.

The biggest change of all, however, was how Matt affected others. More dogs wanted to be around him. More visitors to the shelter wanted to hold him. In the past he didn't have any friends but now he had meaningful friendships with a bunch of dogs, including Bubba. Matt discovered when you are positive you are not the only one who benefits. Everyone around you benefits from your positivity. *When you are positive, you not only make yourself better, you make everyone around you better.*

Positive Energy is Contagious

One day while taking a walk in the yard, Matt and Bubba talked about the impact positivity had on others and Bubba explained that the research shows that heartfelt positive energy is contagious. He said, "It says here in Jade's book that research from HeartMath shows that when you have a feeling in your heart, it radiates to every cell in your body via the heart's electromagnetic field and this energy field can be detected by others, even if they're up to five or ten feet away."

"Is it just positive energy that is contagious?" asked Matt. "After all, it seems like negativity is contagious, too."

"Both positive energy and negative energy are contagious," said Bubba. "Whatever you are thinking and feeling you are projecting to others and impacting them. That's why positivity is not just about you. It's about everyone around you. If you are negative, you impact others in a negative way. If you are positive, you impact them in a positive way. That's why the decision to be positive is soooooo important.

"The simple fact is that each day you have a choice. You can be a germ and infect people with your negative energy, or you can be a big dose of vitamin C and infuse them with your positive energy. Either way, you are influencing people, so it's important to choose to influence people in a positive way."

"It makes a lot of sense," said Matt.

"It's common sense," responded Bubba. "Everyone intuitively knows these things, but because of the daily grind of life and the stress and challenges we face, we forget the simple things we know. We forget that simple is powerful. We forget the powerful impact of a simple smile. We forget the transformative effect our laughter has on others. We forget the influence our positivity has on the world. That's why you need to remember that your positivity not only changes the way *you* feel, but also impacts how others feel. It not only changes your actions, but also impacts the actions of others. I'm not overstating this when I say that your positive energy can and does change the world one person at a time."

Matt knew Bubba was right. Not just because his words rang true, but also because he had personally experienced how others responded to him and his newfound positivity, and how differently they had responded to the old negative Matt.

Positive Boomerang

"Do you know what my favorite thing about positive energy is?" Bubba asked.

"What's that?" Matt said.

"I love the fact that it's like a boomerang," said Bubba.

"What's a boomerang?" asked Matt.

"It's like a Frisbee but shaped differently, so when you throw it, it comes back to you."

"That's no fun. I like to chase Frisbees," said Matt.

"I know, little buddy, but the one thing you don't want to have to chase is positivity—and the great news is that you don't have to. Like a boomerang, when you throw positive energy out to the world, it comes back to you. When you feed the positive dog inside you, you benefit and become more positive yourself. Then you benefit others in a positive way. But it doesn't just stop there. When you impact others in a positive way it comes back to you and feeds your positive dog even more."

"So when I feed others, I feed myself?" Matt asked.

"Yep. That's the beauty of positivity. I love how it works. When you feed yourself, you benefit. When you feed others, you feed yourself too. The more positivity you grow and share, the more it grows and expands and comes back to you." Bubba then looked over his right shoulder and realized that Samantha, a beautiful black lab and Great Dane mix, was listening to their conversation.

"Let me show you how it works," he said, and then told Matt a joke. "If a man wants to know about unconditional love he should lock his mother-in-law, his wife, and his dog in the trunk of his car and drive around for thirty minutes. Then, when he opens the trunk, guess who's happy to see him? That's unconditional love."

Matt and Bubba burst out laughing and, as Bubba expected, Samantha laughed as well. Matt heard Samantha laughing and Bubba explained that this is how positivity works. "Everything we do to be positive contagiously benefits others, and then benefits us even more. When we laugh we cause others to laugh and they experience the same psychological and physical benefits of laughter as we do. And their laughter makes us laugh even more, so positivity grows in us."

"I noticed it's the same with smiling," Matt said. "The more I smile at other dogs the more they smile back."

"That's how it works," Bubba said. "When you share a real smile, you not only produce serotonin in your brain, but the recipient of your smile also produces more serotonin in their brain. So, just by smiling at someone, you give them an antidepressant, and their smile comes back to you and benefits you."

"It also works with friends, doesn't it?" Matt asked.

"Yes it does. When you are positive, positive energy flows out of your heart and attracts others who want to be near and dear to you. Your positivity not only impacts these friends, but these friends also grow your positivity."

Feeding Others

Bubba continued, "One of the most powerful ways to continue feeding the positive dog throughout your life is to be a feeder of others. When you feed others you feed yourself."

"So how do I feed others besides smiling and laughing?" asked Matt. He now had a taste for what positivity could do and was hungry for a double portion of positivity in his life.

"Well a great place to start is by being kind," answered Bubba. "In fact, I believe that changing the world begins with simple acts of kindness. Instead of looking at others as objects you see them as living, breathing forms of life that need your kindness to blossom. Like water and sunlight, your kindness nurtures others and makes the world a better place. A kind word, a kind message, a kind act, and a helping paw can make all the difference, and the feeling you get from sharing kindness actually benefits you the most. In Jade's book there was a study that showed that volunteers who shared their kindness and helped others received numerous health benefits that enhanced their immune system, health, and longevity."

Matt loved the research Bubba shared with him and made a mental note so he wouldn't forget:

> Your kindness feeds others and changes the world.

> Kindness is a gift that is always returned to you.

Love

"We can also build on kindness and feed others with the most powerful form of positive energy there is," Bubba continued.

"What's that?" Matt asked.

"Love. Love dissolves hate, soothes anger, comforts pain, heals relationships, casts out fear, and transforms us and those who receive our love," Bubba answered knowing Matt needed more love in his life.

Matt knew he needed it, too. He had been sharing his positivity with others, but instinctively knew he could share it even more powerfully, if only he knew how. Something was missing, but he wasn't sure what until Bubba said the word *love*.

"You see," said Bubba, "we all want to give and receive love, but many of us are scared to give it because we are afraid of getting hurt."

"I've been hurt in the past, especially before I came here," said Matt.

"I know," said Bubba. "But there's one thing you have to believe: When you share love, it comes back to you. Maybe one dog or person won't return it to you, but if you keep sharing your love with the world it will have such a positive impact on your life that it will come back to you tenfold. There's a great story in Jade's book that talks about a famous opera singer named Pavarotti, who said 'Most singers want the audience to love them, but I love the audience.' This singer has the right approach. Just love everyone. When you love, you don't have to chase love or fear it's going unanswered. When you love, it will fill you up, fill others up, and spill over into every area of your life.

Bubba's words brought tears to Matt's eyes. He thought about his past and, for the first time, found something good about it because it brought him to Bubba. He realized if he had never come to the shelter, he would never have learned the lessons Bubba taught him. Matt was ready to follow his mentor's lead but to truly do so, Matt had to learn one more lesson about encouragement.

Encouragement

Bubba and Matt sat down under a tree and Bubba spoke with more conviction than ever. "There's one more powerful way to feed others that I want to share with you and it is *encouragement!*" Bubba exclaimed. "After all, with so many people and dogs in the world telling us we can't succeed, we need to hear from those who tell us we can. There are enough pessimists and *realists* in the world. The world doesn't need more negativity and impossible thinkers. The world needs more optimists, encouragers, and inspirers. So be an encourager, Matt. Show people you love them by encouraging them. The world needs *you* to speak into the hearts of others and say, *I believe in you. If you have the desire then you also have the power to make it happen. Keep working hard. You're improving and getting better. Keep it up. Great things are coming your way. We've hit a lot of obstacles but we'll overcome. Even if you fail, it will lead to something even better. You're learning and growing.*

"I have found so often that the difference between success and failure is belief, and this is often instilled in us by someone who encourages us. Sure, we'll remember the negative people who tell us we can't accomplish something, but we will always remember and cherish those who encourage us. Decide to be someone who instills a positive belief in someone else—someone who needs to hear your encouraging words—and they'll never forget you."

"Thanks, Bubba," said Matt as he looked at him with hope in his eyes. "I'm definitely going to be a lover of all and an encourager of many. And you know what else?" Matt said as he looked down.

"What?" asked Bubba.

"I know that if we ever get adopted, I'll never forget you."

"I know, little buddy. I'll never forget you, either," said Bubba.

69

Encouragement

No Ordinary Day

Matt woke up a few days later on a morning that started like any other. Matt and Bubba were making funny faces at each other while lying in their cages after breakfast, when a visitor came walking through the shelter. He looked into Matt's cage and said, "What a cute mutt!" Matt thought, *This is it. This is the day.* He was so excited.

But then the man turned around and looked into Bubba's cage, "Hey, old boy," the man said as he reached into the cage and rubbed Bubba's head. The man turned to Barry and said, "That's him." Bubba couldn't believe it. *Dreams do come true*, he thought, slowly wagging his tail. It was his dad! He was alive! Bubba's dad told Barry that he had been in the hospital since the fire and that the first thing he did when he got out was look for Bubba. "I lost everything else in my life, but I knew I would find my Bubba," he said. As Barry opened Bubba's cage, Matt realized it wasn't an ordinary day at all. It was the day Bubba was leaving the shelter.

Bubba stood in front of Matt's cage while his dad signed some papers.

"I always thought you would be the first to leave," said Bubba.

"I know, but I'm really happy for you," said Matt.

"I know you are. I'm happy, too, but I sure am going to miss you and our talks," said Bubba.

"I'm going to miss you, too," Matt said as Bubba's dad put a collar and leash on Bubba and walked him away from the kennels. As Bubba approached the exit, he turned around one last time to see Matt.

"I'm going to miss you more than you know," Matt said quietly under his breath.

Negativity Serves a Purpose

The next few days seemed like an eternity. Each morning Matt woke up and looked into Bubba's empty cage. He tried to go back to sleep, but couldn't. He missed Bubba and his sadness consumed him. He knew it wasn't doing him or anyone else any good to be sad but he couldn't help it. He felt like the positive dog inside him had died.

Then, one night while looking at the stars that filled the dark, clear sky, Matt thought about the negativity he was feeling and realized that negativity does serve a purpose; it helps you see the positive in the world, just as the darkness allows you to see the stars. If you didn't have negative experiences, you would never be able to appreciate the positive ones. If you were never sad, you wouldn't know what it felt like to be happy. If you never felt fear, you wouldn't know what faith felt like. If you were positive all the time, then you wouldn't even know you were being positive because there would be no contrast. You would feel the same all the time.

Matt decided that negativity was a part of life and one should never try to get rid of it completely. After all, if there wasn't a negative emotion such as sadness then he wouldn't know what it felt like to miss his best friend Bubba. If he wasn't able to feel anger, he would have never been able to protect himself from the wild animals he met in the forest before he was brought to the shelter. If he never complained, he wouldn't know how good it felt to be grateful and create solutions.

Matt realized that, ironically, there were positive benefits to be gained from negativity. Negativity actually *helps* you see and appreciate the positive. Negativity forces you to feel those painful emotions so you can recognize and appreciate positive emotions. Negativity builds character and strength when we persevere and overcome it, and facing negative dogs in the world causes us to build positive mental and emotional muscle.

The next day, as soon as he got outside, Matt walked to the spot where Bubba buried Jade's book and dug until he found it. He scooped it up and found the part that supported his belief that negativity was in fact a necessary part of life. According to the book, the key was to have more positivity than negativity. In fact, research by Barbara

Fredrickson showed that the key ratio to remember is three positive emotions for each negative one. People who flourished experienced a ratio greater than three to one. (Three positive emotions to one negative emotion, whereas those with lower ratios—2:1 or 1:1—languished.) The research also showed this to be true for teams at work. Teams that experienced interactions at a ratio greater than three positive to one negative were more productive and higher performing than those with a ratio of less than three to one.

Discovering this ratio shook Matt out of his funk. He was still sad Bubba was gone, but he just needed to turn a negative into a few positives. He needed to experience more positive emotions than negative emotions. He was so inspired he decided that if he ever met Barbara Frederickson, he would lick her hand.

Then he asked himself, "What would Bubba do?" and knew it was time for action.

What Would Bubba Do?

Bubba wouldn't let sadness take him down a spiral staircase of despair. Bubba would turn a negative event into a positive outcome. He would transform a challenge into an opportunity to make a difference. Instead of focusing on what he had lost, Bubba would focus on what could be gained. Matt decided that if Bubba would and could do it, he should and could too.

With Bubba gone, it was up to him to take the lead and share and teach positivity. He didn't know how much longer he would be at the shelter, but he did know that he should make the most of the time he had there. Bubba was proof that dreams could come true, and so Matt kept his hope and vision alive while taking action to feed the positive dog in others.

He mentored other dogs the way Bubba had mentored him—especially the new dogs that came to the shelter and the old dogs that had been there the longest. He found that the young pups were the most open-minded, and once he helped a bunch of them become more positive, he showed the old dogs what positivity could do. He told the old dogs to think like rookies and not let their past experiences hold them back. He told them not to focus on the good old days and believe their best days were behind them. "Instead," he told them, "create your good old days right now and believe that even better days are ahead of you."

Matt taught all of the dogs at the shelter the importance of feeding the positive dog and shared strategies to help them do it. Of course, there were a few that refused to listen or take his advice, but Matt knew that negative dogs were a part of life and he refused to let them bring him down. Instead, they made him stronger and more passionate about helping more dogs be positive. His enthusiasm was contagious and he attracted even more friends than ever.

Matt loved everyone and put his love into action. He listened to other dogs and coached them when they were having problems. He gave constant encouragement and the other dogs accomplished things they never thought possible—they became skilled Frisbee catchers and ran faster than they ever had before. He believed in the other

dogs more than they believed in themselves, and when they found success, they knew his encouragement had made a difference. Matt also made the time to share his appreciation with those who helped around the shelter and recognized the dogs that had become more positive. He found that appreciation, recognition, and mentoring were also great ways to feed the positive dog in others and over time his appreciation, recognition, encouragement, love, kindness, and mentoring increased the positivity in the shelter.

Three months after Bubba left, it was clear that Matt had taken a negative event and turned it into a positive outcome. The little guy had made a big impact. The shelter was transformed and everyone knew it, even the three negative dogs who isolated themselves from everyone else.

As Matt lay in his cage one night dreaming of taking a walk in the park with a family that loved him, he realized that the sad event of Bubba's departure had created an opportunity for him to live with purpose and transform the shelter in so many positive ways.

A Special Day

A few days later, as Matt lay in his kennel thinking about some funny dog jokes, he heard the footsteps of a family as they entered the shelter. He smelled the perfume of a woman, the odor of a man, and the innocence of children. He listened as Barry opened some cages to show the family a few of the dogs.

"One of them will get picked and I will be happy for them," thought Matt. "After all, every dog and owner has already been matched before they even meet." He could hear the family getting closer to his cage but he didn't move. While he had faith, he had also learned not to get his hopes up.

He stayed curled up with his head down until he felt the hand of a little boy reach into his cage and touch the top of his paw. "This one, Daddy," the boy yelled as the parents followed their son to Matt's cage. The man and woman peered into the cage to look at Matt, who decided it was time to stand up and share a smile to brighten their day.

"You like this one?" the dad said to his son.

"Yes, Daddy," the boy said.

Barry took Matt out of his kennel and gave him to the boy who held Matt in his arms. Matt smiled, looked into the boy's eyes, and looked cute as ever, keeping still except for his wagging tail.

"He's not too big and not too little," the boy said.

"He's just right," the mom said, as she lifted Matt from her son's arms and held him in her own. Matt never felt anything like it. He didn't know how to describe it, but it felt like . . . love.

Then, Matt heard the words he had always dreamed of hearing: "We'll take him," the mom said before handing Matt to the boy's older sister.

She looked into Matt's eyes, kissed him on his nose, and said, "I already love you," to which Matt replied, "I've always loved you and I've been waiting for you."

"Let's take him home," the dad said as they walked towards Barry's office to sign the papers. As the family walked towards their car with Matt in the little girl's arms, he couldn't believe it was really happening. He had become a positive dog, fed others, made a difference in the shelter, and now it was time to go home.

Two Positive Dogs are Better than One

A few months later, Matt woke up feeling thankful that he had a family that loved him. He thought about Bubba and all that he had learned about positivity at the shelter, and realized that being positive really is a choice and feeding the positive dog inside you is one of the most important choices you can make. He had become an expert at feeding the positive dog and starving the negative dog and continued to experience the positive benefits in his life. More fun, joy, love, health, and friends made him feel so alive and happy that it was hard to believe he had once been so negative. It was as if the old negative Matt had been another dog. Sure, he still felt negative at times and experienced negative events but these negative emotions and experiences no longer defined him. Now, he was defined by the positive stories he told himself and the positive actions he took to feed himself and others.

As Matt walked to the park with his family, he did what he had done every day since meeting Bubba. He enjoyed a thank-you walk and thought of all the things he was grateful for and prayed for his family and all the dogs at the shelter who weren't adopted yet. He found that gratitude and prayer not only diffused the negative thoughts and emotions he felt but also transformed him from the inside out. They were no longer just strategies to become more positive. They had become who he was.

As Matt and his family approached the park, they crossed paths with a woman and an angry dog that wouldn't stop barking at Matt. Matt didn't respond. He had learned how to deal with negative dogs and wouldn't let them affect him in a negative way. Rather, he saw them as teachers who taught him to be more positive. He knew that to thrive in this world, his positivity had to be greater than the negativity he faced.

When Matt and his family reached the park, Matt was let off his leash and he sprinted in circles as the children chased him. This was what life is all about, Matt thought as he stopped and rolled over on his back so the kids could catch up with him and rub his belly.

When he got to his feet he looked up and saw a man walking through the park with a big dog that had a familiar gait. *Could it be* . . . Matt thought. As the man and dog came closer, Matt recognized the other dog's smell. *I think it is.* He ran up to the big dog and couldn't believe it. It was Bubba, all right.

"I can't believe it's you," said Matt. "I thought I'd never see you again."

"I can't believe it's you, either," responded Bubba. "I often wondered if you were adopted and now I know my little buddy realized his dream. I'm so thrilled for you."

"So, what are you doing here?" asked Matt.

"We just moved to the neighborhood."

"Do you like it?" asked Matt.

"I like it a whole lot better now," said Bubba. "As I always say, two positive dogs are better than one."

"You got that right," said Matt. "The neighborhood is about to get a double boost of positivity."

And as Bubba's dad and Matt's family met each other, the two positive dogs played tag and reminisced about the fun they had learning to feed the positive dog. They didn't know it while they were at the shelter, but what had seemed like the worst events of their lives served as preparation for the life they now enjoyed. They had become positive dogs and the world was a more positive place because they were in it.

The End

Feed the Positive Dog
Action Plan

You've read the story and now you know the importance and benefits of feeding the positive dog. The research shows that we can develop more positivity in our lives and share it with those around us, at work and at home. The more we feed the positive dog the bigger it gets and the stronger it becomes. The key is to take action. In this spirit, I have created an 11-day action plan with a daily strategy to feed yourself with positivity. The purpose of this plan is to help you experience more positivity in your life and provide you with simple strategies to take charge of your positive thoughts and emotions. My hope is that when you are done with the plan, you will choose the strategies and exercises you like best and make them habits. For example, I take a thank-you walk every day and it has become my favorite positivity booster. I also ask my children, each night before bed, about their success of the day. When you finish the plan you'll be able to create your own plan and incorporate one or more of the following strategies into your life and work. Let's start feeding the positive dog.

Day 1: Take a Thank-You Walk

It's simple, it's powerful, and it's a great way to start feeding the positive dog. How does it work? You simply take a walk . . . outside, in a mall, at your office, on a treadmill, or anywhere else you can think of, and think about all the things, big and small, that you are grateful for. The research shows you can't be stressed and thankful at the same time so when you combine gratitude with physical exercise, you give yourself a double boost of positive energy. You flood your brain and body with positive emotions and natural antidepressants that uplift you rather than the stress hormones that drain your energy and slowly kill you.

Note: If you love the thank-you walk, feel free to do it every day.

Day 2: A Day of Gratitude

A number of studies show that grateful people tend to be more optimistic, which improves immune function, heart health, and happiness levels, according to Robert Emmons, a gratitude expert and professor of psychology at the University of California–Davis. In a nutshell, being thankful is good medicine and necessary for a positive life.

Today as you live, work, interact, shop, commute, and do everything else, turn off the negative news and, throughout the day, identify all the things you are grateful for. To help you do this, you may want to implement the *get to* instead of *have to* strategy. You may also want to create a gratitude journal, on paper or using your mobile device, and make a list of the things you are grateful for.

Day 3: More Smiles and Laughter

They say that children laugh about 400 times a day, while adults laugh only about 25 times. Perhaps we need to be more like children and smile and laugh more. Research shows that smiling produces more serotonin in your brain and laughter reduces stress, increases your immune system, and causes your body to release "feel good" endorphins. Today I want to encourage you to find enough humor in your life to make you laugh and smile for at least 10 minutes. Here are some ideas to smile and laugh more today:

- Watch funny videos on YouTube (www.youtube.com).
- Watch one of your favorite funny movies.

- Get a joke book and share the funniest jokes with a friend.
- Watch a funny television show.

Day 4: Celebrate your Success of the Day

According to sports psychologist Jim Fannin, the last 30 minutes of every waking day are recorded and replayed that night by our subconscious minds 15 to 17 times. This replay occurs five times more often than any other thought at any other time. Thus, it's important to go to bed thinking positive thoughts. If you go to bed thinking and feeling like a champion, you'll wake up thinking and feeling like a champion—optimistic and ready to win.

Today, before you go to bed celebrate your success of the day. Identify the one great thing about your day—the one great conversation, accomplishment, or win that you are most proud of. Or identify the one person you helped most today or the one thing that made you smile. Focus on your success, and you'll look forward to creating more success tomorrow.

Day 5: Spend Time with Positive People

Research shows that the old adage that money doesn't buy happiness is true. However, being rich in friends certainly does make a difference. According to a survey from the National Opinion Research Center, the more friends you have the happier you are. Other studies show that close relationships promote health, support longevity, and enhance positivity. So, today, make time to connect with the positive people in your life and take the time to strengthen your relationships with them. Get together with an old friend, call a loved one, or take action to make a new friend. Positive people make us feel more positive so spend time with them today.

Day 6: Share the Gift of Kindness

Sonja Lyubomirsky, author of *The How of Happiness*, has been researching different techniques and strategies to increase happiness. Not surprisingly, one of the successful happiness boosters is performing acts of kindness, such as volunteering for a charity, opening the door for someone, feeding the homeless, or taking your elderly neighbor grocery shopping. Lyubomirsky has found that by engaging in five acts of kindness in a single day (the impact is more powerful if performed in one day rather than spreading five acts over five days) participants in her studies experience a measurable boost in happiness.

Make today a day of kindness and engage in five acts of kindness. Some acts you will be able to schedule and plan, while other acts can be more spontaneous. The key is to perform five acts in one day. For ideas visit:

www.giftofkindness.com.

Day 7: Smell the Roses

According to Barbara Frederickson, author of *Positivity*, research shows that spending time in nature boosts your positivity, especially when the weather is good. Anyone who has been to the beach, taken a walk through a forest, or spent time fishing on a lake knows how good it feels to be immersed in nature.

Today, take the time to smell the roses and spend some time in nature. Take your lunch break in a nearby park. Ride your bike to the beach. Take your kids hiking in the mountains. Go fishing at a nearby lake. Exercise with a friend in a park. If you love golf consider a visit to the golf course as beneficial as a trip to the park so long as you take the time to enjoy the air, the trees, and the green grass. Connect with nature and connect often. It will feed your positive dog.

Day 8: Take Out your Telescope

I often talk about a telescope when encouraging people to create a big-picture vision for their future and dream about the life they want to create. The telescope represents our dream for the future and, according to Barbara Frederickson, research shows this is a simple way to boost positivity.

Today dream about the life you want to create. Write down your big-picture vision. What does it look like? What are you doing? What do you hope to accomplish? What difference do you want to make? What is your mission and purpose? Spend some time visualizing the future you want to create. Then write down your vision, dreams, and goals.

Day 9: Make a Gratitude Visit

Martin Seligman, PhD, the father of positive psychology, suggests that we write a letter expressing our gratitude to someone. Then we visit this person and read them the letter. His research shows that people who do this are measurably happier and less depressed a month later.

Today make a gratitude visit to an old boss or mentor, a friend who helped you through a tough time, a family member, or someone who has made a positive difference in your life.

Day 10: Lose Yourself in the Moment

When we are engaged in an activity in the present moment and doing something that interests us, we feel more positive.

Today, choose an activity that will engage, interest, and energize you. Play an instrument, dance to your favorite dance music, paint, play a sport, surf, plant some flowers, play checkers or chess, read a good book, or choose another positive activity that will allow you to enjoy the present moment and feed your positive dog.

Day 11: Be a Coach

Coaches bring out the best in others. The best coaches mentor, encourage, praise, inspire, and lead with optimism and positivity.

Today, feed others and yourself with positivity by being a coach. Instead of complaining about what others are doing wrong, start focusing on what they are doing right. Praise them, encourage them, love them, recognize them, and inspire them to be their best. You'll help others feel great and you'll feel great too.

Every Day: Pray

Scientific research shows that daily prayer reduces stress; boosts positive energy; and promotes health, vitality, and longevity. When you are feeling stressed to the max, stop, be still, and plug in to the ultimate power to recharge.

Here are a Few Ways to Starve the Negative Dog:

- Turn off the news.
- Don't participate in gossip.
- Turn complaints into solutions.
- Identify the negative stories you tell yourself and replace them with positive stories.
- Replace fear with faith.
- See negative people as teachers who help you become more positive.
- Choose positive words instead of negative words.
- Sign up for Jon's free weekly positive tip at www.JonGordon.com.

The Positive Pledge

Read the pledge, choose to be positive, and make a positive impact on the world.

I pledge to be a positive person and a positive influence on others.

I promise to be positively contagious and share more smiles, laughter, encouragement, and joy with those around me.

I vow to stay positive in the face of negativity.

When I am surrounded by pessimism, I will choose optimism.

When I feel fear, I will choose faith.

When I want to hate, I will choose love.

When I want to be bitter, I will choose to get better.

When I experience a challenge, I will look for opportunity to learn and grow.

When faced with adversity, I will find strength.

When I experience a set-back, I will be resilient.

When I meet failure, I will fail forward toward future success.

With vision, hope, and faith, I will never give up and will always move forward toward my destiny.

I believe my best days are ahead of me, not behind me.

I believe I'm here for a reason and my purpose is greater than my challenges.

I believe that being positive not only makes me better, it makes everyone around me better.

So today and every day I will be positive and strive to make a positive impact on the world.

Sign, print, and share the pledge at:

www.feedthepositivedog.com.

Two Positive Dogs are Better than One

Share the positivity with others.

Visit www.FeedthePositiveDog.com to:

- Participate in the free *Positive Dog* video book club.
- Print and share free *Positive Dog* posters.
- Watch positive videos.
- Share the *Positive Dog* principles with others.
- Learn more about the research featured in the book.
- Learn more about our positive training programs.
- Discover Jon Gordon's Positive University.

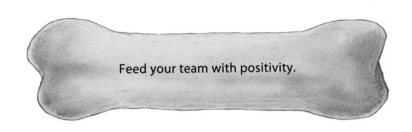

Feed your team with positivity.

If you are interested in leadership, sales, and team-building keynotes or training programs based on *The Positive Dog* principles contact The Jon Gordon Companies at:

Phone: (904) 285-6842
E-mail: info@jongordon.com
Online: www.JonGordon.com
Mail: 830-13 A1A N.
Suite 111
Ponte Vedra Beach, FL 32082

Sign up for Jon Gordon's weekly e-newsletter at:

www.JonGordon.com

 Facebook.com/JonGordonPage

 @JonGordon11

About the Illustrator

Artist-Animator-Musician

Donald Wallace has dedicated his entire life to art and music. He applies his artistic abilities in all areas of the media producing cartoons, illustration, animation, movie concept art, and graphic design. Whether designing and producing for computer animation, animating in the traditional hand-drawn style, creating digital illustration for the print and Internet markets, or developing cartoon characters and concept design, there isn't much he hasn't experienced in his career. Artistically, he has been involved in four music video productions, directed art and animation for several CD-ROM games, and designed, produced, and directed hundreds of commercials for television. Musically, he is currently composing instrumental works and developing a musical play. He lives and works in Portland, Oregon, with his wife Kelly, and their cat, Toonces. He can be reached at 503-224-9660.